Thank you to the children who suggested their favourite amazing facts: Tom Bourne-Cox, Lyra Chilton, Rudy Chilton, Calla Mackenzie, Evan Mackenzie — C.B.

Written by Catherine Brereton.
Illustrations by Chris Dickason.
Front cover design by Thy Bui.
Red Shed would also like to thank author Clive Gifford for use of some content from *Fake News*.

First published in Great Britain in 2021 by Red Shed, part of Farshore

An imprint of HarperCollins*Publishers*
1 London Bridge Street, London SE1 9GF
www.farshore.co.uk

HarperCollins*Publishers*
1st Floor, Watermarque Building, Ringsend Road, Dublin 4, Ireland

Copyright © HarperCollins*Publishers* Limited 2021

ISBN 978 0 0084 9220 5
001
Printed and Bound in the UK using 100% Renewable Electricity
at CPI Group (UK) Ltd.

A CIP catalogue is available from the British Library.

MIX
Paper from
responsible sources
FSC™ C007454

AMAZING FACTS EVERY 9 YEAR OLD NEEDS TO KNOW

RED SHED

Whether you love animals or adventure, science or sport, you'll find LOADS of weird and wonderful facts ...

Which animals vote by sneezing?

What was the biggest shark ever?

What does space smell like?

Which baby animals cover themselves in poo for protection?

Read on to find out the answers and lots more awesome information ...

Sea otters hold hands
while they're sleeping.

They sleep floating on their backs, and often
link paws so they don't drift apart. They also
have the thickest fur of any animal, which
keeps them warm in water.

Capybaras eat their own poo and they sometimes act like chairs!

These close relatives of guinea pigs are the world's largest rodents and eat their own poo like rabbits do. They swim in the Amazon river most of the day, but when they're standing up or resting, other animals like to sit on them.

One tiny rainforest frog goes to great lengths to look after its babies.

The strawberry poison dart frog dad pees on the eggs every day to keep them damp. Then when the tadpoles hatch, the mum carries them all the way from the floor up into a pool high in the treetops.

The Amazon rainforest is home to around 40,000 different plant species.

There are also hundreds of different animals, birds, reptiles and amphibians, thousands of types of fish and many millions of invertebrates, including 2.5 million different insects!

There's a species of bacteria that only lives in hairspray.

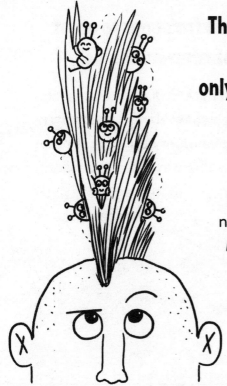

In 2008, scientists in Japan discovered a tiny rod-shaped bacteria, which they named *Microbacterium hatanonis*. It has only been found living in hairspray.

Scientists don't know for sure why we have fingerprints.

Experiments have shown they don't improve grip. One theory is that the grooved texture makes them much more sensitive than smooth skin.

Goosebumps are a reminder of our ancient ancestors.

Goosebumps are what you see when your fine body hair stands on end. Millions of years ago when our ancestors' furrier hair stood up, it made them look more threatening to predators.

A man once ate an entire aircraft.

Between 1978 and 1980, Frenchman Michel Lotito ate a whole Cessna 150 light aircraft! Nicknamed Monsieur Mangetout (Mr Eat-Everything), he had parts of the plane cut into bite-sized pieces, then gobbled them down.

Chimpanzees know what to eat if they are ill.

These clever apes choose particular leaves or seeds if they are feeling poorly, and this helps them get better.

Some starfish stomachs get to work outside their bodies.

Instead of swallowing food into their stomach, they splurge the stomach out of their mouth and around the food, squirt digestive juices into the food and slurp it back up into their body later.

Every pet dog in the world today is descended from wolves.

Scientists have worked out that today's dogs can all trace their family tree back to grey wolves living in Siberia, Russia, around 23,000 years ago.

The border collie is the most intelligent pet dog breed.

African wild hunting dogs vote to make decisions – and do so by sneezing.

They get together in the pack and if most of them sneeze, especially the pack leaders, they will head off to start hunting.

The gold and jewels in Tutankhamun's famous tomb weighed over 1,200kg.

That's as much as 120 solid gold bars. It included gold statues, gold furniture, elaborate jewellery and a dazzling gold and jewel mask.

Ancient Roman soldiers rubbed themselves with stinging nettles to keep warm.

And the ancient Egyptians used the tingle-causing plants to treat arthritis. Don't try this at home!

The first prehistoric turtles didn't have shells.

Turtles have been swimming in the seas for around 210 million years. But before that they didn't have shells or beaks. We know this because of a 230-million-year-old fossil, discovered in 2018.

The largest ever insect was a dragonfly with wings as big as a magpie's.

The dragonfly *Meganeuropsis permiana* had a wingspan of 70cm and lived among the dinosaurs 300 million years ago.

Giant prehistoric sea scorpions called eurypterids were even bigger, at 2m long.

The prehistoric shark megalodon was three times longer than the biggest shark today.

Every year there is a music
festival in Florida, United States,
that is held underwater.

Musicians dressed as mermaids and mermen play unusual instruments, such as a fishy-looking trombone or a shark-shaped harp.

The songs are watery – such as 'Yellow Submarine' and 'Octopus's Garden' – and it's all to draw attention to the need to protect coral reefs.

Children in the United States were sometimes sent away by post.

Some parents figured out it was cheaper to send their child by Parcel Post than pay for a train ticket. In 1931, five-year-old Charlotte May Pierstorff was posted 100km to visit her grandmother. She had stamps on her coat and a label with the address on.

A reindeer once lived on a submarine for six weeks.

In 1941, during World War II, a British submarine accepted a present from the Soviet Navy – an adult reindeer! She was named Pollyanna and later went to live at London Zoo.

One of the biggest, most expensive pieces of scientific equipment in the world once broke down because of a mischievous animal.

The machine was the Large Hadron Collider and it stopped working in 2012 when a stone marten – a cousin of the weasel – chewed through an electric fence, causing a power cut.

The Large Hadron Collider is a giant machine as big as a city.

It is an enormous cylinder, 27km in diameter, and it's deep underground beneath the Alps mountains in Switzerland and France.

The LHC is looking at things so tiny they're smaller than atoms.

Tiny particles called atoms make up everything in the Universe. But they in turn are made up of even tinier particles, called subatomic particles, and the LHC is investigating these.

In Toronto, Canada, people hardly need to go outside in winter.

A network of underground walkways means they can get around the city centre's shops, workplaces and attractions without braving the sub-zero temperatures that last for months on end.

The coldest place in the world to live is Oymyakon, Russia.

This village is the coldest settlement where people live all year round. It is regularly –50°C in winter and once dropped below –71°C!

**A storm on the
planet Jupiter has lasted
for more than 300 years.**

The storm is called the Great Red
Spot and is 16,350km across –
bigger than the whole of
planet Earth!

**There was an even bigger storm
on the planet Saturn.**

From December 2010 to August 2011, a storm
raged on Saturn that circled the whole planet and
was large enough to cover 10 to 12 Earths.

Earth's tallest mountain is actually Mauna Kea in Hawaii, United States.

You may know that Mount Everest is the tallest place on Earth, at 8,850m above sea level. But Mauna Kea's summit is 4,207.3m above sea level plus around 6,000m under the sea, making it more than 10,000m tall overall.

Male mandrills like to show off their stripy faces and flash their colourful bottoms.

These are the biggest monkeys of all.
The strongest, most powerful mandrills
in a group have the brightest red and blue
faces and red bottoms.

Mandrills have longer fangs than lions do.

Some capuchin monkeys have invented their own insect repellent.

These clever monkeys, which live in South American rainforests, rub their fur with poisonous millipedes, and this works like a bug spray, keeping biting insects away.

In chilly Iceland, you can enjoy a warm outdoor swim all year round.

The country has many hot springs, heated by geothermal energy. This is heat from deep in Earth's crust and in Iceland it rises up to just below the surface. Geothermal energy provides much of Iceland's electricity, too.

Iceland has no mosquitoes.

Iceland is growing by about 5cm per year.

The tectonic plates of Earth's surface are moving apart and new land is appearing between them. In Iceland you can clearly see it happening.

Most of Earth's plates are moving apart by just 2.5cm a year (about as fast as your fingernails grow).

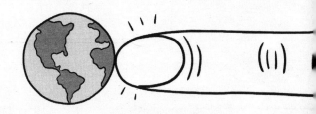

Our galaxy, the Milky Way, contains around 300 billion stars.

It is a spiral-shaped galaxy and our Sun is one of the stars near one of the arms of the spiral.

The centre of our galaxy tastes like raspberries!

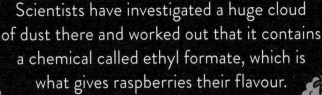

Scientists have investigated a huge cloud of dust there and worked out that it contains a chemical called ethyl formate, which is what gives raspberries their flavour.

Other regions of space taste like burnt steak.

Many of the astronauts at the International Space Station have reported a meaty taste!

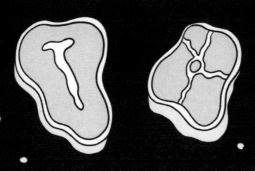

Scientists think that Titan, one of Saturn's moons, probably smells of gasoline.

During the Great Fire of London in 1666, writer Samuel Pepys buried a cheese!

As the fire raged, Londoners rushed to save their precious possessions and flee. Pepys buried money, documents, wine and a large wheel of Parmesan.

In 1698 in Russia, Tsar Peter the Great brought in a tax on beards.

The emperor wanted to modernise Russia and thought beards were old-fashioned. Men either had to shave or pay a tax. They would get a token to show they had paid.

A kung-fu expert in China cuts people's hair while standing upside down!

Wang Xiaoyu is a barber in Changsha who stands on his head as he works.

The International Goldfish Championship takes place in Fuzhou, China, every year.

Thousands of goldfish are judged on their breed, shape, colour, size and gracefulness when swimming.

Goldfish do NOT have very short memories.

In fact they can remember quite well. Scientists have done experiments that make us think they can recognise and remember certain sounds and spot their owners. Why not give your pet a wave!

The Roman Emperor Commodus loved gladiator fights so much he joined in himself!

He was known for being brutal, a bit stupid and a disastrous emperor. And of course he fixed the fights so he would win!

The Canary Islands are NOT named after canaries.

Lying off the coast of North Africa, they were named Canariae Insulae, meaning 'islands of dogs', by the ancient Romans – possibly after sailors spotted wild dogs there.

A cake once went to court to prove it wasn't a biscuit.

In the UK, the makers of Jaffa Cakes argued over whether the teatime treats were biscuits or cakes. They produced a giant one to show it really is more of a cake.

People first added milk to tea to prevent their dainty china from breaking.

In the 18th century, when tea first became popular in Britain, drinkers put milk in the cups so that boiling water wouldn't crack them. In east Asia, where tea comes from, it is served black.

Scientists are trying to create vaccines in bananas.

Most vaccines come in the form of injections. But scientists are working on genetically engineering bananas so they can hold the vaccine instead. Injection or banana split?!

The oldest thing on Earth smells like rotten peanut butter!

In 2020, scientists were examining a meteorite that landed on Earth in 1969. They found specks of dust that were 5–7 BILLION years old and these smelled a bit like rotten peanut butter.

Fear of that feeling of having peanut butter stuck to the roof of your mouth has a name: arachibutyrophobia!

Peanut butter can be made into diamonds.

Using enormous pressure – up to 280,000 times that of the air pressing on you now – and some very expensive equipment, German scientist Dan Frost has turned peanut butter into a diamond!

In the 17th century in England, singing Christmas carols was against the law.

The strict government banned any form of Christmas celebrations and demanded that 25 December should be a normal, serious working day.

An African trio is the longest-running girl band of all time.

Singing sisters Amal, Hadia and Hayat Talsam from Sudan have been performing for 45 years.

The composer Scarlatti wrote his 'cat fugue' tune after his cat walked across his piano keyboard.

In 2015, Canadian astronaut Chris Hadfield recorded a whole music album mainly in space.

**Wildlife lovers on safari
look for the 'big five' African
animals . . . but there is also
a less famous 'little five'.**

The 'big five' are the elephant, lion, rhinoceros, leopard and Cape buffalo.

The 'little five' are the elephant shrew, ant lion (a type of insect larva), rhinoceros beetle, leopard tortoise and buffalo weaver (a type of bird).

A carnivorous plant in Borneo has evolved into a tree shrew toilet!

The rainforest pitcher plant's nectar attracts the tree shrews, which slurp up the nectar and poo into the plant. The plant eats insects too, but the poo is its main food.

An Amazon forest fungus turns ants into zombies!

Amazingly, a killer fungus gets into a carpenter ant's brain and forces it to climb up a tree, bite on a leaf and then die. The fungus then bursts out of the zombie ant's head.

Ninjas had a way of walking called 'deep grass rabbit walking'.

Ninjas were stealthy secret assassins in Japan in the 14th to 16th centuries. They were experts at disguise and needed to move about silently and out of sight.

A Japanese student of ninja history got top marks for handing in a blank paper!

Eimi Haga copied a method used by ninjas to send secret messages. She made an invisible ink out of soya beans and left her teacher a clue that said 'heat the paper' . . . and her essay appeared.

A book in Argentina was printed with disappearing words.

The Book That Can't Wait was printed with a special ink that fades away 60 days after the book is first opened. The idea is to get people to read it quickly!

The longest underground railway in the world is in Seoul, South Korea.

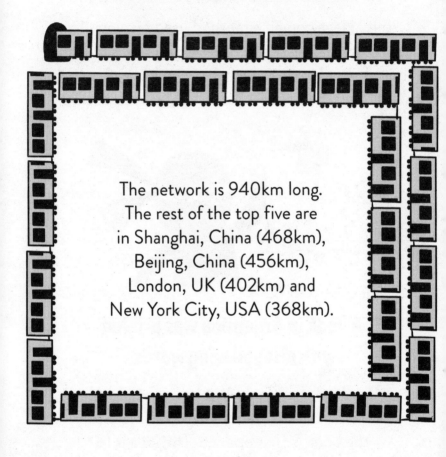

The network is 940km long. The rest of the top five are in Shanghai, China (468km), Beijing, China (456km), London, UK (402km) and New York City, USA (368km).

The world's shortest scheduled passenger flight is just 2.7km long.

The short hop is between the Orkney islands of Westray and Papa Westray in Scotland, UK, and usually takes as little as 90 seconds!

Around 750 years ago, an explorer called Marco Polo met some unicorns and thought they were ugly.

They were actually rhinos.

Rhino horns are made of the same stuff as our fingernails.

The material is called keratin and it is also found in animal hooves and birds' beaks and claws.

Sailors once thought manatees were mermaids.

The manatee, or sea cow, is a swimming mammal that lives in warm waters including in the Caribbean. Manatees sometimes swim upright like mermaids would, and European travellers in the 15th century thought that's what they were.

Victorian seaside visitors often had to use an elaborate machine to go for a dip.

When the seaside holiday became popular in the 18th and 19th centuries, rich ladies had to be taken into the water in a little wooden changing cart so no one would see them on the beach in their swimwear.

Seaside rock and lots of other famous sweets were invented in Victorian times.

The driver of the first long-distance car trip was also the first car mechanic.

Bertha Benz made a 106-km car trip in Germany one day in 1888. Along the way she fixed several things that went wrong, and invented brake pads.

In 1896, a car made by the Benz company was the first to receive a speeding ticket. It was zooming through Kent, England . . . at 12km/h!

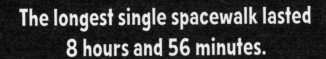

The longest single spacewalk lasted 8 hours and 56 minutes.

The record was set by US astronauts James Voss and Susan Helms in 2001. Russian cosmonaut Gennady Padalka has spent the longest time in space overall – 878 days in total.

The incredible International Space Station (ISS) was built in space.

It took 115 space flights to build it and cost around US $100 billion. It is powered by giant solar panels containing 262,400 solar cells!

It takes the ISS just 90 minutes to orbit Earth, meaning it sees 16 sunrises and sunsets every day.

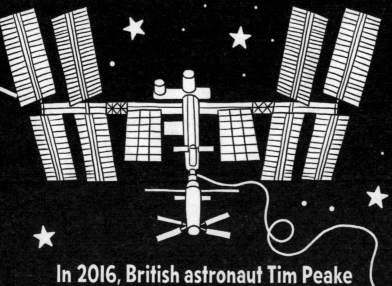

In 2016, British astronaut Tim Peake competed in the London marathon – on a treadmill in the ISS!

A news report in April 1930 said 'There is no news.'

It wasn't an April Fool – the BBC radio news on 18 April 1930 consisted of these few words followed by 15 minutes of piano music.

A photo of a shark attacking a helicopter fooled millions on the internet.

In 2001, a photo of this amazing attack went viral, but it was a hoax. Someone had merged a photo of a helicopter doing training exercises with a photo of a shark just leaping up out of the water.

Snow on the pyramids was another fast-moving hoax.

In 2013, a picture went viral that claimed to show snow on the Great Sphinx statue in Egypt for the first time in over 110 years. The snow was real but the scene was a tiny model of the statue in Japan.

'Fake News' was Word of the Year in 2017.

The term, for false or misleading information described as news, had been around since the 1890s but was used so much by politicians in 2017 that the *Collins English Dictionary* chose it as the word that had jumped the most in popularity.

A real-life dragon has poisonous spit and eats its own babies.

The world's largest lizard, the Komodo dragon, kills its prey with a poisonous bite. It can eat animals as big as deer and water buffalo, but also eats newly-hatched dragon babies.

The babies cover themselves in poo to try to protect themselves.

Wasps use spit to make paper for building.

They scrape up shavings of wood and mix it with their saliva to create paper, which they use to build their nests.

Your teeth are the hardest substance in your body.

Tooth enamel is even harder than bone. Teeth are fixed into your skull but they are not part of it – and the skull is not just one bone but 21 bones fused together.

A tooth will NOT dissolve in a glass of fizzy drink overnight.

Fizzy drinks do contain acids that will dissolve teeth (though not as much of them as there is in orange juice). And although these acids *will* eat away at your teeth, it will take much longer than one night.

Swallowed chewing gum doesn't really take seven years to digest.

In fact you don't digest it at all! Any sugars and flavourings get absorbed and digested like any other food, but the gum itself passes straight through.

Your mouth produces a litre of saliva every day.

The man who made Frisbees popular is now a Frisbee.

The plastic flying discs really took off in the 1960s when 'Steady' Ed Headrick redesigned them and set up an International Frisbee Association to arrange tournaments. In 2002, he died and his ashes were mixed with plastic to make some memorial Frisbees.

The first vacuum cleaner was so big it had to be pulled along by a horse-drawn wagon.

It was built in 1901 by British inventor Hubert Cecil Booth, and was soon being used in Buckingham Palace.

In 1907, American janitor James Murray Spangler invented the first hand-held version. His cousin's husband, Henry Hoover, was so impressed that he bought the rights to the machine, which is why we often call it a 'Hoover' now.

Badgers build a separate toilet area as part of their underground setts.

Badger setts can spread across an area of up to 60m^2 and are made up of many rooms and tunnels. Badgers spend a lot of time repairing, cleaning and rebuilding them.

Termites build towers complete with heating and cooling systems.

Termite mounds, home to millions of termites, contain chambers like chimneys, which blow cool night air around during the heat of the day.

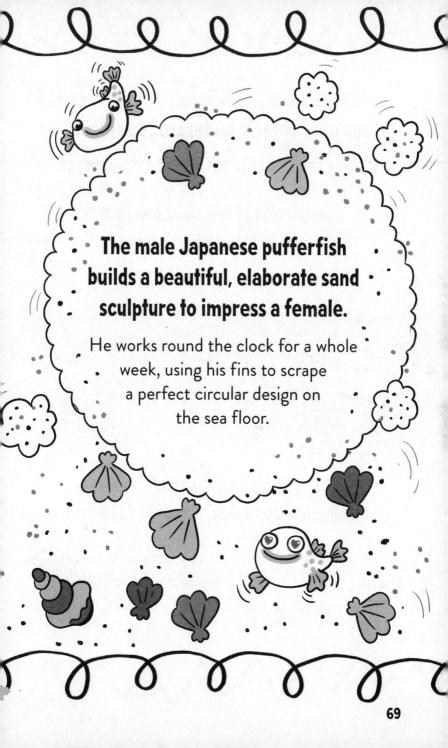

The male Japanese pufferfish builds a beautiful, elaborate sand sculpture to impress a female.

He works round the clock for a whole week, using his fins to scrape a perfect circular design on the sea floor.

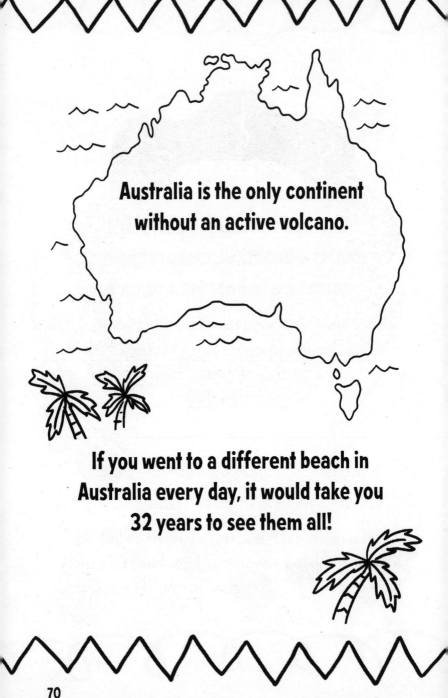

Australia is the only continent without an active volcano.

If you went to a different beach in Australia every day, it would take you 32 years to see them all!

Australia's platypus is one of the world's strangest mammals.

It is a mammal but it lays eggs, has a bill like a duck and has a venomous bite. Now scientists have discovered it has glow-in-the-dark fur, too.

Plants can talk to each other and the world around them.

When attacked by insects, plants release different chemicals. Some of these poison the insects and some send out perfumes to attract animals that will eat the insects. Other plants nearby can pick up the scent and do the same!

A cactus called 'the wandering devil' travels from place to place.

It creeps along the ground, growing at the top and dying at the bottom, travelling 60cm a year.

Some species of bamboo burst into flower everywhere around the world at the same time.

The most popular food in the world is ... grass.

Most human diets are based on rice, wheat, maize, barley, oats, rye or millet, which are all kinds of grass.

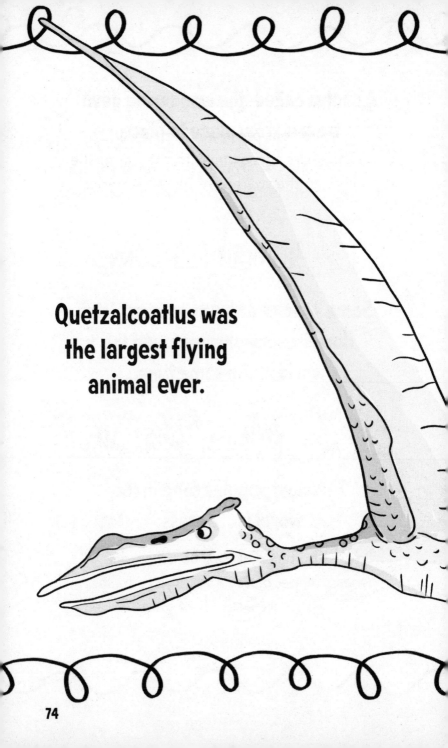

Quetzalcoatlus was the largest flying animal ever.

This enormous pterosaur lived around 65 million years ago, along with the last of the dinosaurs, in the swamps of North America.

It had a wingspan of around 11m – about twice as long as a giraffe is tall.

Your brain comes up with about 12,000–16,000 thoughts a day.

Most of them are the same thoughts you had the day before. Hmmm, where's my breakfast?

Reading out loud uses different circuits in your brain to reading silently.

The blood you see on TV is not as gory as you might think.

Fake blood on screen (or for scary Halloween costumes) is made up of a variety of ingredients such as sugar syrup, red and blue food colouring and cornflour. But in the days of black-and-white films, these red concoctions didn't show up well. So lots of famous scary movies used chocolate syrup!

Albert Einstein came up with some of his most brilliant scientific ideas while checking other people's inventions.

Einstein was the 20th century's most famous scientist, who made several important discoveries about how the Universe works. He made many of these while working at a patent office in Bern, Switzerland, reading and checking descriptions of new inventions.

Ada Lovelace invented computer programs before any computers had been built!

In the 1840s, young Ada was friends with the English mathematician Charles Babbage, who was working to create a computer. His invention was not actually built, but Ada wrote a detailed set of instructions for it, which is now considered to be the first computer program.

A Hollywood movie star helped invent WiFi.

Austrian-American actress Hedy Lamarr enjoyed inventing as a hobby alongside acting. In the 1940s, she teamed up with a composer friend George Antheil and they invented the radio technology that WiFi is based on.

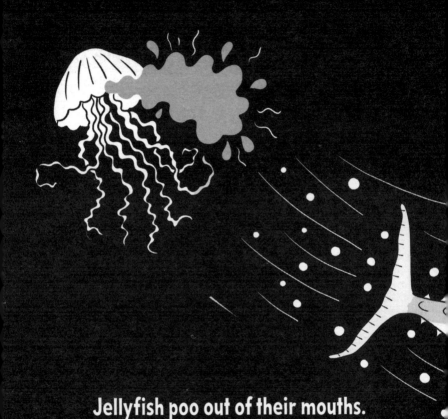

Jellyfish poo out of their mouths.

They have just one opening that serves as both
a mouth and an anus. They also have no brain,
no heart or blood, and many have no eyes.

A tuna fish swims so fast it can hardly breathe.

Fish breathe through their gills, absorbing oxygen from water as it flows over the gills. But a tuna swims so fast that this doesn't work. It speeds along with its mouth open and absorbs oxygen from the water that flows into its mouth.

The biggest dinosaur egg was three times the size of an ostrich egg.

Hypselosaurus eggs were 30cm long and 25cm wide. Ostriches, the largest birds today, have eggs 15cm long and 12.5cm wide – enough to fit 24 hens' eggs inside.

Ostrich babysitting is a real job.

The job of watching over ostrich chicks may sound adorable, but mainly involves trying to stop the aggressive chicks fighting and pecking each other or running off.

An ostrich's kick is powerful enough to kill a lion!

The youngest Olympic gold medalist was just 13 years old.

American diver Marjorie Gestring won gold at the Olympics in Berlin, Germany, in 1936. But the youngest known Olympian of all, Greek gymnast Dimitrios Loundras, was just 10 when he won bronze in Athens, Greece, in 1896.

American swimmer Trischa Zorn won 12 gold medals in a single Paralympics.

She has won 41 Paralympic medals in total, more than the top Olympic medal-winner, another American swimmer Michael Phelps, on 28.

Paul the octopus became a worldwide celebrity for predicting the outcome of football matches.

The octopus, from an aquarium in Germany, correctly predicted the outcome of all of Germany's matches in the 2010 World Cup. Each time, he was shown two boxes with the flags of the teams playing, and chose one to take food from. And each time, that team won!

There are trees growing on Earth that have been to the Moon.

On the Apollo 14 mission in 1971, astronaut Stuart Roosa took 500 tree seeds with him as an experiment to find out how space would affect them. He later planted the seeds and around 400 'Moon trees' were sent around the world – and are growing today.

Astronauts have seen the Moon's 'dark side'.

People talk about the 'dark side of the Moon' when in fact all of the Moon gets its fair share of light from the Sun. But the same side always faces Earth so the only way to see the other side is to send space probes or astronauts there.

Astronauts grow in space – a 1.8-m-tall person may come home 5cm taller!

The Artemis space mission aims to land the first woman on the Moon in 2024.

Bats make different sounds to talk about different subjects.

They use very high-pitched squeaks and clicks to find prey. But they also make different singing and chattering noises to talk to each other about food, sleep and other bats.

Pigeons can find their way by sensing Earth's magnetic field.

It's like having their own built-in compass.

Horses can recognise human feelings and get upset if they see an angry face.

Scientists have found that they can tell the difference between a smile and an angry grin, even in a photograph.

Bumblebees can tell if another bee has just visited the flower they're feeding on.

A bumblebee gives off a tiny electrical charge as it buzzes around. Then another bumblebee can sense the charge the first one has left behind.

A huge football ground in El Salvador was the scene for the world record for the most people brushing their teeth at once.

An amazing 13,380 people took part in the tooth-shining event at the Estadio Cuscatlán in the city of San Salvador in 2005. In 2019 in India, 26,382 people smashed the record.

A football club in Brazil had a colourful way to get fans to donate blood.

In 2012, the Vitória football club removed the usual four red stripes from their shirts. They promised to put the red back if fans donated blood to local medical centres. Donations rose and soon the red stripes were back.

Orang-utan babies are the oldest babies in the world.

Orang-utans, one of our closest relatives, stay with their mother for years as she teaches them all the skills they need. They are still babies – feeding on mum's milk – until they are six years old.

Amazing Facts Every 6 Year Old Needs To Know

Ming the mollusc was one really old animal.

An ocean quahog (a type of clam) named Ming was caught in 2006 and was estimated to be 507 years old! Scientists knew this because clams have age rings, like trees do.

The oldest ever person lived to be 122.

Jeanne Calment from Arles, France, was born in 1875 and was still cycling at the age of 100.

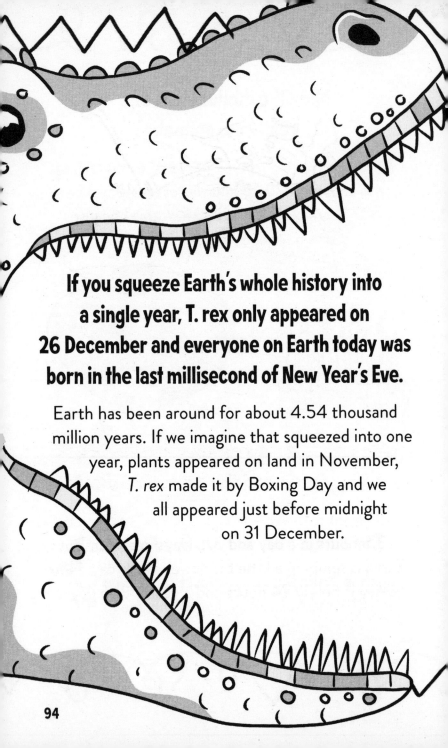

If you squeeze Earth's whole history into a single year, T. rex only appeared on 26 December and everyone on Earth today was born in the last millisecond of New Year's Eve.

Earth has been around for about 4.54 thousand million years. If we imagine that squeezed into one year, plants appeared on land in November, *T. rex* made it by Boxing Day and we all appeared just before midnight on 31 December.

When dinosaurs were alive, the world was spinning faster and the days were shorter.

Over 65 million years ago, there were around 23.5 hours in a day and 370 days in a year. But Earth is spinning a little bit slower every day. Now a day is nearly 24 hours and a year is 365 days.

A type of frog in Brazil has spots on its bottom that look like eyes.

When a predator comes along, the Cuyaba dwarf frog sticks out its bottom to scare the predator away.

An eel once burst out of a heron's stomach – still alive!

Herons are expert fishers, but the huge eel was too much for one poor bird in 2020. The eel burrowed out of the bird's stomach and through its belly to escape!